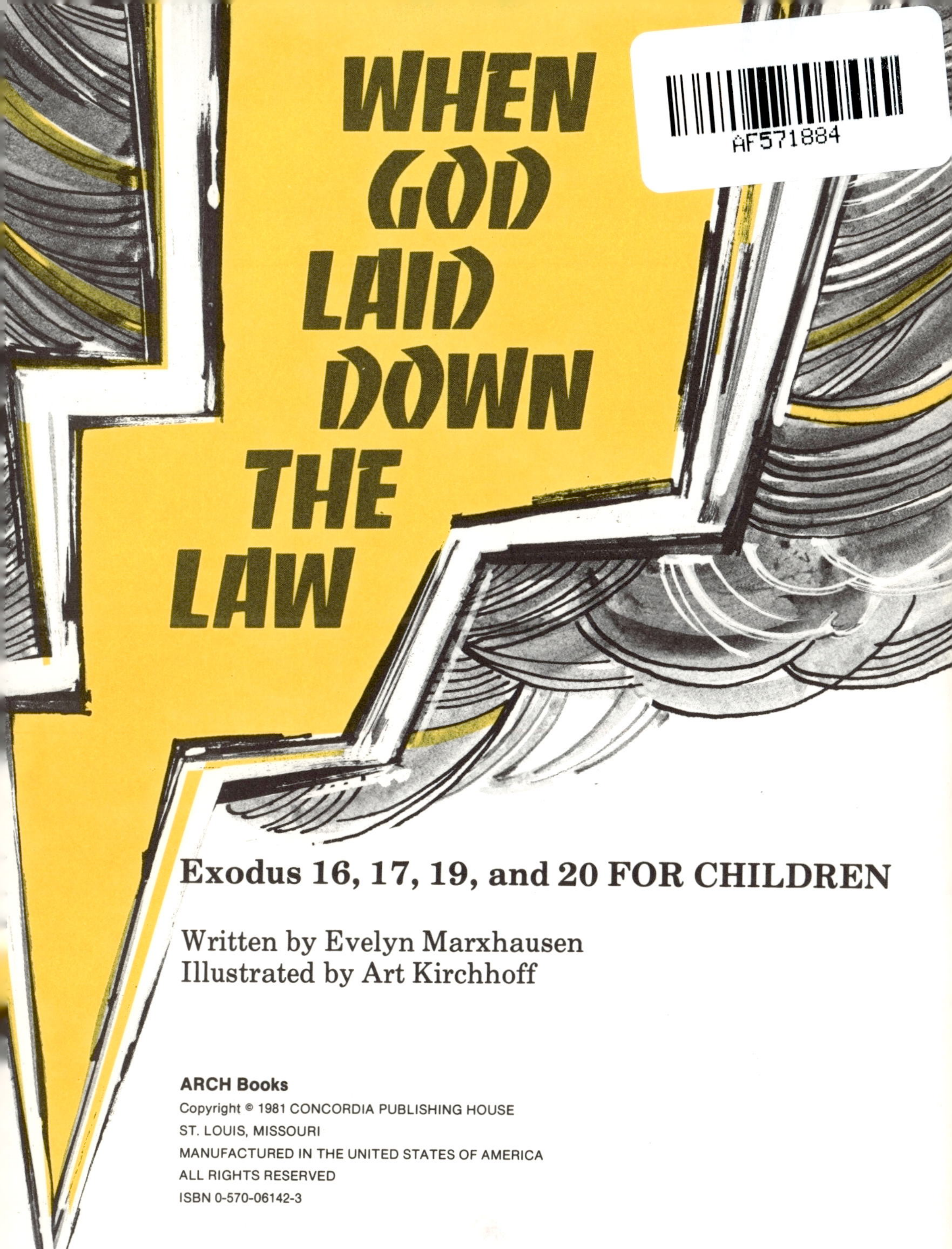

WHEN GOD LAID DOWN THE LAW

Exodus 16, 17, 19, and 20 FOR CHILDREN

Written by Evelyn Marxhausen
Illustrated by Art Kirchhoff

ARCH Books

ST. LOUIS, MISSOURI
MANUFACTURED IN THE UNITED STATES OF AMERICA

ISBN 0-570-06142-3

Do you remember Moses,
The mighty man of God,
Who led God's chosen people
Through the Red Sea with his rod?

And how Moses led the people
Through all the desert land,
How God always protected them
With His almighty hand?

And when they had no water,
They all began to cry,
"We are thirsty! Give us water
Or we will surely die."

Then God told Moses once again
To take his special rod
And strike a rock so that water flowed
By the mighty power of God.

And when they had no food to eat,
He sent down little flakes
Which they could pick up from the ground
And bake into some cakes.

So you see, God loved these people,
For He did all these things.
He led them out of Egypt
As though on eagles' wings.

And He wanted them to love Him,
To obey all His commands
And not forget what He had done;
And He promised them new lands.

When they had traveled many months,
They came to a big hill;
God said: "Moses, come up here.
I must tell you My will."

So one morning on the mountain
There was a terrible storm
With lightning, thunder, and a cloud
And loud blasts from a horn.

So Moses knew that God was there.
He climbed up to the rim;
And from somewhere on that mountain
He heard God talk to him.

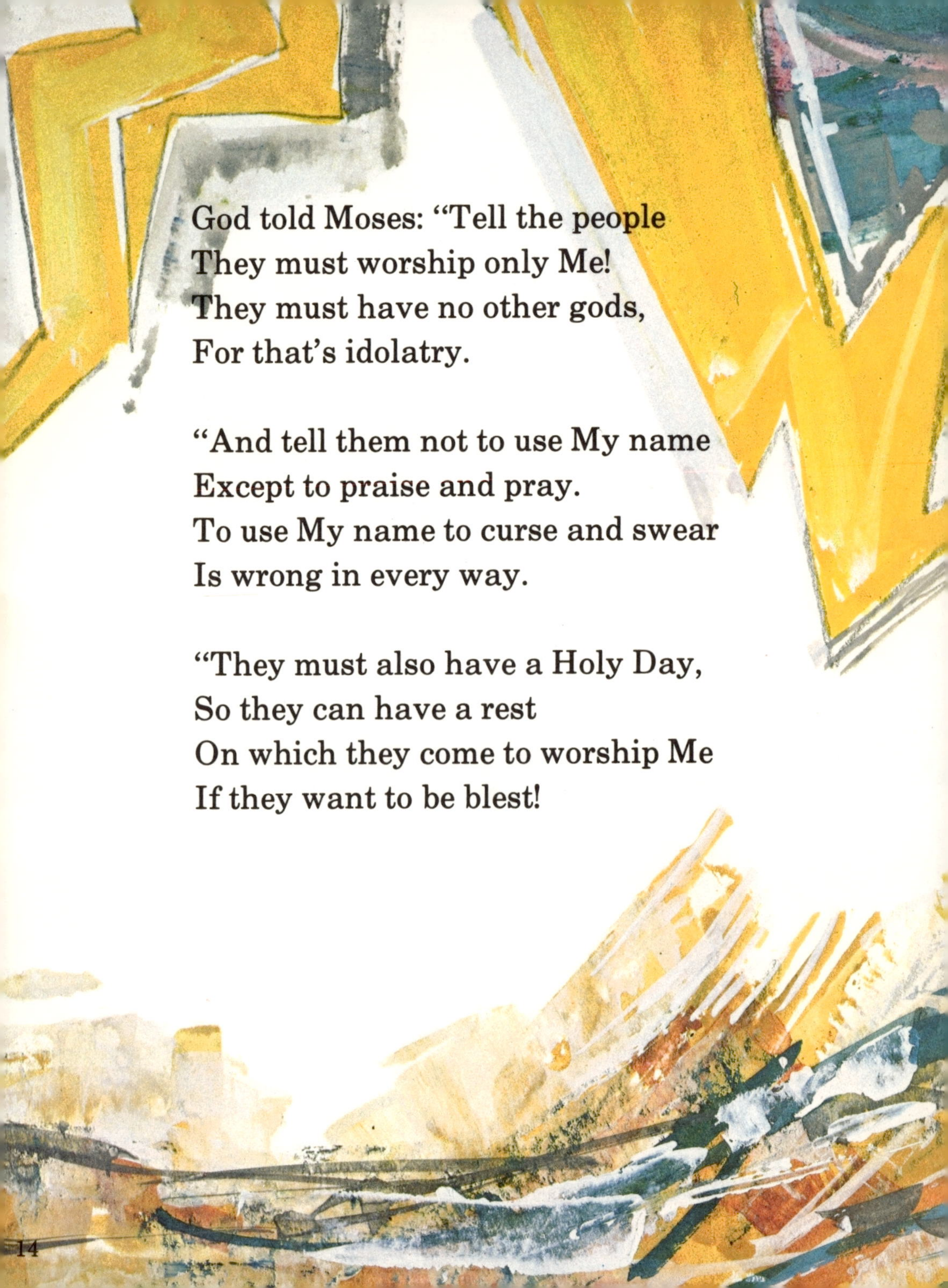

God told Moses: "Tell the people
They must worship only Me!
They must have no other gods,
For that's idolatry.

"And tell them not to use My name
Except to praise and pray.
To use My name to curse and swear
Is wrong in every way.

"They must also have a Holy Day,
So they can have a rest
On which they come to worship Me
If they want to be blest!

"They must honor both their parents.
They must love them and obey;
Then they will have a long, good life
And be happy every day.

"They must not kill or hurt someone,
Nor commit adultery;
They must not steal or tell a lie,
For this is sin, you see.

"They must not always want to have
Other people's property,
But be content with what is theirs—
Not be filled with jealousy."

So these are the Commandments
That God laid down that day;
And He told Moses: "Tell the people
They must listen and obey."

When the people saw the mountain
Begin to quake and quiver,
When they heard the roaring thunder,
They began to shake and shiver.

But do you know what happened then?
The people soon forgot;
They did not keep God's laws at all
But began to sin a lot.

They cried, "Moses, Moses, please tell God
We will promise to be good;
We promise we'll obey His laws
And do the things we should."

God became extremely angry
At those people there below;
He said: "I'll have to punish them,
But I still love them so.

"Someday I'll send a Savior
Who is Jesus, My own Son;
He'll lead a perfect life for them,
Keep My commandments—every one!

He'll suffer all the punishment
For the bad things they have done;
Then I'll forgive them all their sins
If they trust Jesus, My own Son."

Just like those people long ago
We, too, do not obey;
We, too, forget about God's laws
And walk in our own way.

Although we may try very hard
To obey God and be good,
We know we simply cannot
Be as perfect as we should.

But God still loves us very much
And we will be forgiven;
For it's not through laws, but by His grace
That we will go to heaven.

DEAR PARENTS:

As the opening verses relate, God had done great things for the Israelites before they ever reached Mount Sinai. Over and over again He had demonstrated His great love for His covenant people.

In giving the Law, God revealed His holy, eternal will—valid for us and our God-ignoring society as well as for ancient Israel.

Like the Israelites, we promise to avoid sin and do good; but, again like them, we repeatedly fail to keep that promise. So all of us—we and our children—stand in need of the forgiveness God has provided through the perfect obedience and the suffering, death, and resurrection of His Son Jesus, our Savior.

Teaching the Commandments (what they demand and what they forbid—and all of them do both) is surely of value. But let God's goodness and forgiveness be your chief emphasis when you discuss this story with your child. Only the Gospel message of His love can supply the proper motivation for our and our children's continuing efforts to do God's will and keep His Commandments as best we can.

THE EDITOR